PHILADELPHIA

A PICTORIAL SOUVENIR

CAROL M. HIGHSMITH AND TED LANDPHAIR

PHILADELPHIA

A PICTORIAL SOUVENIR

CRESCENT BOOKS

NEW YORK

THE AUTHORS WISH TO THANK THE FOLLOWING FOR THEIR GENEROUS
ASSISTANCE IN CONNECTION WITH THE COMPLETION OF THIS BOOK:

Dennis B. Arwood and Craig R. Baclit, Elliott-Lewis Company
Julie P. Curson, Philadelphia
Pamela and David Dembe, Philadelphia
Eve and David Eagan, Jenkintown
Meryle Fischer, Philadelphia Convention and Visitors Bureau
Don and Lynn Martin Haskin, Philadelphia
Rosemarie and Marc Kuhn, Plantation, Florida
Joyce and Robert Mozenter, Chestnut Hill
Hyman Myers, Philadelphia
J. Mickey Rowley, Top of the Tower
John Todd, Chestnut Hill
Robert Williams, Pennsylvania Convention Center Authority

———

PAGES 2–3: The skyline of "colonial" Philadelphia has changed dramatically in recent years.

This 1999 edition is published by Crescent Books®,
an imprint of Random House Value Publishing, Inc.,
201 East 50th Street, New York, N.Y. 10022.

Crescent Books® and colophon are registered trademarks of
Random House Value Publishing, Inc.

Random House
New York • Toronto • London • Sydney • Auckland
http://www.randomhouse.com/

Printed and bound in China

Library of Congress Cataloging-in-Publication Data
Highsmith, Carol M., 1946–
Philadelphia / Carol M. Highsmith and Ted Landphair.
    p.   cm. — (A pictorial souvenir)
ISBN 0-517-20488-6
1. Philadelphia (Pa.)—Pictorial works. I. Landphair, Ted, 1942–   .
II. Title. III. Series: Highsmith, Carol M., 1946–   Pictorial souvenir.
F158.37.H54   1999   98–38557
    974.8´11´00222—dc21   CIP

8   7   6   5   4   3   2   1

———

Project Editor: Donna Lee Lurker
Designed by Robert L. Wiser, Archetype Press, Inc., Washington, D.C.

FOREWORD

Philadelphia has become one of America's most dynamic and appealing tourist destinations. This was not always the case. Of course, people always came to the nation's birthplace to see Independence Hall, but for the longest time, Philadelphia was often overlooked in the roll call of great American cities. Part of the reason was that it was overshadowed by New York, less than one hundred miles away. The other reason was the traditional, self-effacing Quaker attitudes, such as frowning on self-promotion, that continued to pervade the city's character. After all it was "the Quaker City" founded by William Penn. No one should stand out, so Philadelphia did not try.

In the nineteenth century, Philadelphia was called the "Athens of America." And it boasted people like Benjamin Franklin, a brilliant and eccentric inventor, publisher, scientist, diplomat—and wit—as one of its illustrious citizens. But immigrants from Italy, Poland, and Russia poured into the city as Philadelphia became the "Workshop of the World" and the hub of America's Industrial Revolution. They changed the face of the city's neighborhoods and its latter-day reputation was that of a gruff, blue-collar town.

Penn named his city "Philadelphia"—Greek for "City of Brotherly Love"—and many of its citizens personify the gruff exterior and warm heart of Rocky, the character from the smash series of *Rocky* movies about a Philly boxer who makes it big. "Philadelphians . . . open to you the longer they get to know you," says longtime local columnist Don Hasidic, and Condé Nast *Traveler* magazine called Philadelphia "the nation's friendliest city."

Old Philadelphia is as charming as ever, and Independence Hall and the Liberty Bell remain its magnet. Other popular downtown sites include the Fireman's Hall Museum; Elfreth's Alley, the oldest continuously occupied street in Philadelphia; the house where local seamstress "Betsy" Ross reportedly designed the first Stars and Stripes flag of the new nation; and Bookbinder's Restaurant, which opened in 1865.

South Philadelphia, with its five-block-long Italian Market full of fresh produce, cheeses, and a hundred other delicacies, also offers some of the nation's best Italian restaurants. Center City is dominated by the massive Second Empire-style City Hall with its famed Alexander Milne Calder statue of William Penn. City Hall—the grandest and most expensive public building in the world when built in 1894—was designed to house the city administration, council, and municipal courts. Near City Hall stands the restored Reading Terminal, high in the esteem of nostalgic Philadelphians, which has been modernized and converted into the East Coast's second-largest convention center.

In 1996, *USA Today* gushed, "the city is alive with culture, visual art, music, theater and dance." The city is the home of such nationally renowned cultural attractions as the Philadelphia Orchestra, the Barnes Foundation Gallery, and the Philadelphia Museum of Art. And each spring, the Philadelphia Flower Show—the "Olympics of Gardening"—attracts more than 250,000 visitors. And greater Philadelphia has more colleges and universities—eighty-two—than the Boston and Baltimore areas combined.

Philadelphia is smaller but stronger than it was a half-century ago. It is still tinkering with its mix of modern and historic, cultured and brash. And the joke is on anyone who underestimates the City of Brotherly Love.

The Department of the Interior erected a postmodernist "ghost" structure (above) to mark the spot in Center City where Benjamin Franklin built his three-story house and print shop. Beneath "Franklin Court" is the Franklin Museum, whose exhibits recount many of the eclectic interests of the city's most famous "Renaissance man." In 1775, the Second Continental Congress convened in Independence Hall (right), the Pennsylvania Colony statehouse. A year later, delegates adopted the Declaration of Independence and appointed George Washington commander-in-chief of the Continental Army. It was to Independence Hall, too, that the founders returned to draft and approve the constitution for the new nation in 1787.

Elfreth's Alley (opposite), created in 1703, is the nation's oldest continuously occupied street. Row houses, which appeared in the late eighteenth century, were occupied primarily by local craftsmen. Jeremiah Elfreth, for whom the alley is named, was a black smith. Wealthier business investors in the Pennsylvania Colony lived in Society Hill townhouses. Major David Lenox, president of the Bank of the United States, occupied this 1759 house (left) on Spruce Street. Later, government leaders lived in Society Hill when Philadelphia was the nation's capital. The neighborhood, close to Independence Hall, declined during Philadelphia's industrial boom and was a slum by the 1950s when "urban renewal" targeted the area. By the 1980s, Society Hill had regained its cachet. I. M. Pei was among the architects who designed towers and townhouses in the revitalized neighborhood.

Samuel Blodgett Jr.'s 1797 First Bank of the United States (left) was commissioned by Secretary of the Treasury Alexander Hamilton soon after the nation adopted a single currency. William Strickland designed the Merchant's Exchange (above)—the first stock exchange in the country. After the exchange dissolved during the Civil War, vendors kept food stalls around the building for more than a century. Bookbinder's Restaurant (overleaf), which opened in 1865 and became the restaurant of choice of Philadelphia and visiting celebrities, is now a landmark. "Booky's," as some natives call it, is famous for its soups. The family sold this original Bookbinder's in the 1940s and opened Bookbinder's Seafood House on South Fifteenth Street.

THE GAMEWELL JOKER

If you were to send an alarm from the box at Independence Hall, which is numbered "1776", it would be registered on the "Gamewell Joker" system you see here. The box would send a series of electrical taps to this system. A single tap, a pause, then seven more taps, pause, seven taps, pause and six taps, indicating the number 1776.

The brass gong would ring out the taps and they would also be registered on the paper tape. A quick glance at the "tar" board in the center and firefighters would know if they were to respond and where.

When this firehouse was active, it is said certain fire horses could recognize the signals from the "Joker" and ...

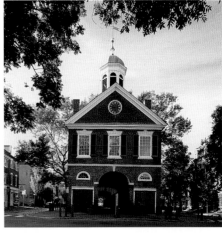

The Fireman's Hall Museum (left) is located in the 1876 Engine Company No. 8 firehouse on Second Street. Benjamin Franklin (who else?!) organized the city's first fire company in 1736, and in 1871 the city's volunteer groups merged into the nation's first professional fire department. Among the museum's displays is the "Joker" fire alarm system. The exhibit is wired in such a way that visitors will hear today's fire alarms as they would throughout the city. Head House Square (above) was Society Hill's new market when it opened in 1745. Vendors rented spaces, first from a private company, then from the city, which took over the operation in 1772. Volunteer firefighters used some of the houses as stations, and fire companies met upstairs to socialize.

15

Sculptor Joe Brown designed two football-player statues, including this punter (opposite)—as well as two baseball-player statues—that are mounted outside Veterans' Stadium in South Philadelphia. There are also hockey and basketball statues outside the Spectrum, the stadium's companion building in the sports complex. Outside the smaller arena, too, is Thomas Schomberg's bronze statue of Rocky Balboa (left), the hero of the series of Rocky boxing movies. In South Philly, too, is the colorful Mummers Museum (overleaf), which displays fascinating accoutrements and historical remnants of the annual New Years Day "Shooters' and Mummers' Parade." The first part of the spectacle's name derives from an early Swedish custom of firing off pistols and muskets to join with bells and noisemakers in heralding the new year.

Daly Street (opposite) is a quintessential lane of row houses in the Whitman neighborhood of South Philadelphia. Neighbors socialize outdoors as well as in each other's homes. Eateries like Jim's Steaks (left)—as in Philly cheesesteak hoagies, not filet mignon—and Lorenzo's Pizza Parlor (above) are part of the lively scene on eclectic South Street. The popular shopping corridor declined into tawdriness, but it has made such a comeback that South Street is often compared favorably with New York's Greenwich Village. Most shops, galleries, and restaurants—of which there are more than one hundred on this single short street—are open evenings, and the street is packed on weekends as well.

Four generations of the Ochs family meat business—three that are pictured (left)—have been prominent stall-holders at the Reading Terminal Market, which was beautifully refurbished in the early 1990s. Lena Zook (above), a young Amish woman from Lancaster County, serves fresh-baked soft pretzels—a time-honored Philadelphia delicacy—at another stand in the market. The last train to depart the old Reading Terminal upstairs (overleaf) pulled out on the evening of November 6, 1984, bound for Lansdale and carrying six hundred admirers of the old railroad and its flagship depot. The train shed was preserved and incorporated into the city's sweeping new Pennsylvania Convention Center.

In 1865, Philadelphia's Union League club—formed by wealthy donors to the Union cause in the Civil War—moved into a spacious Second Empire building (left), designed by John Fraser. The Philadelphia Academy of Music (above), which opened just before that war, is home to the nonpareil Philadelphia Orchestra. Architects Napoleon Le Brun and Gustave Runge modeled the academy after La Scala in Milan. Fanatical about acoustics, they directed that the building sit empty for a year, without a roof, so the walls could properly settle. Celebrated Philadelphia architect Frank Furness designed the building that houses the Pennsylvania Academy of Fine Arts (overleaf)—the nation's oldest art museum and school.

Previous Pages: Kennedy Plaza is one of the sites of "Phillyfest," a series of free, noontime concerts and other entertainment that are a Philadelphia tradition. The gavel used to dedicate the cornerstone of Philadelphia's Masonic Temple (left)—one of the world's most impressive Masonic structures—on June 24, 1868 was the one that George Washington, a Mason, had used to lay the cornerstone of the United States Capitol in Washington seventy-five years earlier. One of the Philadelphia Masons' own, twenty-seven-year-old James Windrim, designed the Norman structure. The interior features seven lodge halls—including an Egyptian Hall decorated with hieroglyphics copied from eight temples in Egypt—representing different periods in world history. The Cathedral of Saint Peter and Saint Paul (above), in grand Italian Renaissance style, was completed after twenty-two years of construction at Logan Square in 1888.

33

Claes Oldenburg designed the forty-five-foot-high Clothespin *(right)* at Centre Square, across from City Hall. The sculpture was a radical departure from the traditionalist statuary abundant elsewhere in the city. Centre Square was one of five parks laid out by Philadelphia's original city planner, Thomas Holme. The others are Rittenhouse, Franklin, Logan, and Washington. Not since City Hall, at the turn of the twentieth century, and the PSFS Building, during the Great Depression of the 1930s, had both Philadelphia's skyline and its image so dramatically changed as they did when Willard G. Rouse's One and Two Liberty Place towers *(opposite)* rose in 1987 and 1990, respectively. The buildings broke the unofficial covenant against exceeding the 491-foot height of "Billy Penn's" hat atop City Hall.

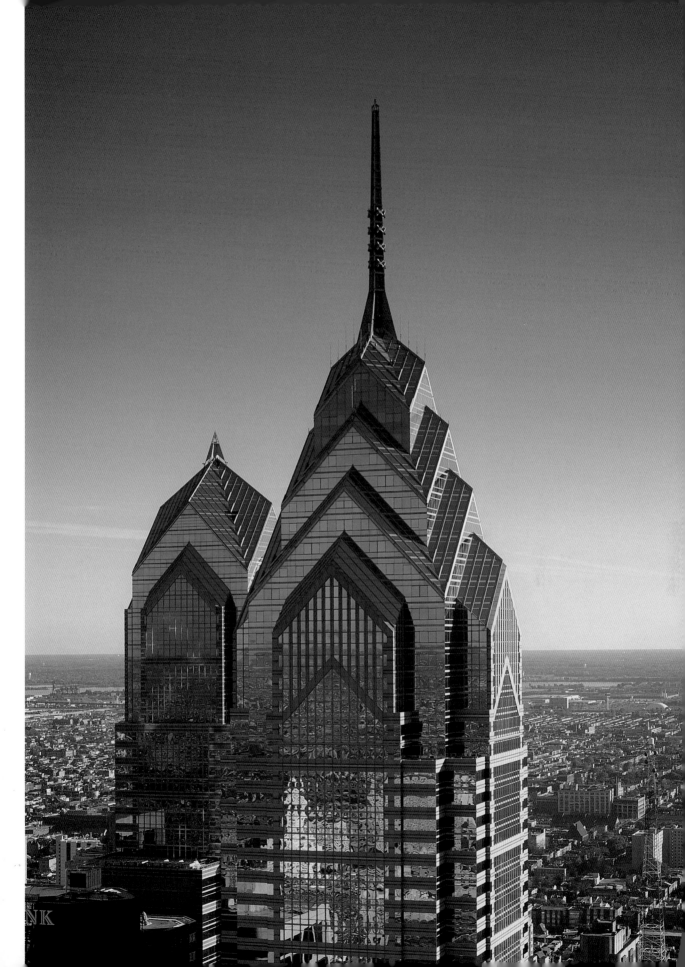

While the skyline of Philadelphia has changed radically, with several soaring skyscrapers added in the 1990s, City Hall (left) has remained the focus of the Center City. The laborious restoration of City Hall in the late 1990s took years to reach many of the intricate details of this massive Second Empire struc- ture, including these Alexander Milne Calder sculptures (above) in a projected corner pavilion. Calder did not just design cherubs and other classical figures; he also executed the cher- ished twenty-seven- ton, bronze rendition of William Penn that stands atop the four-acre building.

Philadelphia has
become a medley of
shining skyscrapers
and historic treasures.
The William Penn
statue (opposite)
above the City Hall
clock tower no longer
has the highest aerie.
The Schuylkill, the

"River of Revolutions"
(above), winds from
the heart of Philadel-
phia to Valley Forge.
Along the way are
museums, mills and
farmsteads, Revolu-
tionary War forts,
waterworks, limestone
quarries, an indus-

trial canal, a twenty-
two-mile bikeway,
and sites such as Mill
Grove, the first
American home of
naturalist John J.
Audubon. A plethora
of museums, monu-
ments, circles, and
squares line the

stately Benjamin
Franklin Parkway
(overleaf) connecting
the Philadelphia
Museum of Art and
City Hall. "Phila-
delphia's Champs
Elysées" was designed
by French-born archi-
tects Jacques Greber

and Paul Philippe
Cret during the
nation's effusive "City
Beautiful" movement
of the early twentieth
century. Cret also
designed another
"Ben Franklin":
the bridge over the
Delaware River.

Logan Circle (opposite), began as one of William Penn's city squares that was turned into a traffic circle after World War I. It was named for James Logan, Philadelphia mayor, judge, mathematician, and land speculator, who administered Pennsylvania Colony for William Penn. Alexander Stirling Calder, son of the City Hall sculptor, designed Swann Memorial Fountain's bronze figures, which represent the city's three principal waterways: the Delaware and Schuylkill rivers, and Wissahickon Creek. Along the Benjamin Franklin Parkway, Auguste Rodin's statue The Thinker (left) announces the Rodin Museum, which exhibits many of the French artist's masterworks. The entryway was inspired by Chateau d'Issy—Rodin's own home in Meudon, France. The museum, a gift to the city from Jules Mastbaum, was dedicated a month after the Stock Market Crash of 1929.

43

An equestrian statue of George Washington (above), which stands on Eakins Oval before the Philadelphia Museum of Art, is one of more than twenty-five grand statues on the Benjamin Franklin Parkway. The monument, designed by German sculptor Rudolf Siemering, was originally placed in Fairmount Park in 1897 and moved to the parkway in 1928 as part of the effort by civic leaders to adorn Philadelphia in the trappings of a great world city. Herman Atkins MacNeil designed the marble pylons on the 1927 Civil War Soldiers and Sailors Memorial (right) at the entrance to the parkway. Battles from that war are inscribed on the memorial's walls that face the Museum of Art.

The Philadelphia Museum of Art (opposite) was built on Faire Mount Hill. Eli Kirk Price, who led the museum's fundraising drive, shrewdly directed that its two side wings be com-pleted first, knowing that Philadelphians would not leave the central temple unbuilt. Its prodigious set of stairs is known around town as the "Rocky Stairs" because boxer Rocky Balboa, hero of the Rocky movie series, trained by ascending seventy-two of the ninety-nine steps. The museum displays its world-class collection—including a statue of Diana (above), created by sculptor Augustus Saint-Gaudens as a weathervane for the first Madison Square Garden in New York—in two hundred galleries. Downhill from the museum, along the Schuylkill River, is the Greek Revival-style Phila-delphia Waterworks (overleaf). Designed by Frederick Graff, the building was the first steam pump-ing station of its kind in the nation.

Memorial Hall (opposite) in Fairmount Park was the Great Hall of the 1876 Centennial Exposition, which touted the young nation's industrial achievements. It and four other of the fair's halls were created by Hermann Schwartzmann, a Fairmount Park engineer who had never designed a building. Philadelphia's art museum was housed in Memorial Hall until the new museum opened in 1926. The winged horses (top right) flanking the building's entrance were created by Augustus Saint-Gaudens, who would later sculpt much of the statuary of the 1893 World's Columbian Exposition in Chicago. Fairmount Park is dotted with artistic delights like Frederic Remington's statue (bottom right).

Philadelphia judge
Joyce Mozenter and
her husband Bob,
an eminent defense
attorney, are inveter-
ate joggers and two
of the thousands of
Philadelphians who
savor Fairmount

Park's wooded won-
derland (above). At
almost nine thousand
acres, with more than
one million trees and
one hundred miles of
nature trails, it is the
world's largest land-
scaped urban park.

The red covered
bridge, built in 1855,
is the last covered
bridge remaining
within a large
American city. The
bronze lions (oppo-
site) outside the
Philadelphia Zoo are

a favorite reconnoi-
tering spot. Founded
in 1859, the Zoological
Society of Philadel-
phia was the first zoo
in the nation, and its
children's zoo, which
opened in 1938, was
also a first. So were

the births of the
first orangutans,
chimpanzees, and
cheetahs to be born
in America. More
than sixteen hundred
animals live on the
Philadelphia Zoo's
forty-two acres today.

Thousands of commuters and Amtrak passengers board and arrive at 30th Street Station (opposite and above) in West Philadelphia each day. The monumental structure, completed in 1934 and beautifully restored in 1991, once even had a landing deck for small planes on its concrete roof. By locating the station across the Market Street Bridge over the Schuylkill River, the Pennsylvania Railroad deflected not just rail traffic, but also attention and urban development, away from Center City for the first time. The railroad turned to a Chicago architectural firm—Graham, Anderson, Probst, and White—to design the massive, neo-classical building. Because steam locomotives were fast fading from use, the architects were able to design the terminal above tracks, with smokeless electric trains in mind. The station's magnificent interior has been the setting for scenes in several movies, including Witness *and* Blow Out.

The University of Pennsylvania moved from downtown to West Philadelphia in 1870, but it was another twenty-five years before it had its first dormitory, the Quadrangle (opposite). The building, which is actually thirty-nine interconnecting structures around several courtyards, is rich in ornamentation, including its much-loved gargoyles. Long a men's dorm, the Quadrangle now houses approximately fourteen hundred undergraduates of both sexes. There are three statues of the school's founder, Benjamin Franklin, on the historic Ivy League campus. This 1899 bronze on a granite base (top left) was designed by John J. Boyle. In 1893, Philadelphia banker Anthony J. Drexel provided the seed money for the University City neighborhood's other center of higher education, the Drexel Institute of Art, Sciences, and Industry (bottom left), now Drexel University.

In 1912, on his Fonthill estate in Doylestown, Henry Chapman Mercer opened the Moravian Pottery and Tile Works (opposite), whose elaborately decorated product was used in structures as far from Philadelphia as Graumann's Chinese Theater in Hollywood. The tile works is now a museum where tile is still produced. George Washington maintained his headquarters in a converted 1774 farm-house (left) at Valley Forge, now a National Historical Park. His men endured the frigid winter of 1777–78 in more than a thousand hastily constructed log cabins.

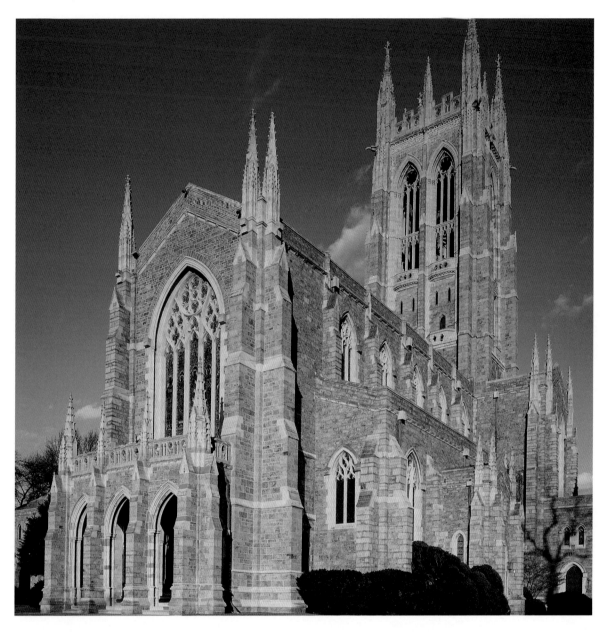

The 1883 Saint Thomas of Villanova Church (opposite) is on the Villanova University campus, but it is a parish church, not the university chapel. Much of the funding

for its construction came from Irish Catholic immigrants working in the hotels and summer homes of prominent Philadelphia families. Building of the

Church of New Jerusalem's Bryn Athyn Cathedral (above), overlooking the Pennypack Valley, began in 1914 and continued for several decades using the

painstaking medieval guild system of construction. Longwood Gardens (overleaf), established by Pierre S. Du Pont in Kennett Square near Brandywine, is one of

the world's most spectacular horticultural displays. More than eleven thousand plants can be found within Longwood's 1,050 outdoor acres and 20 indoor gardens.

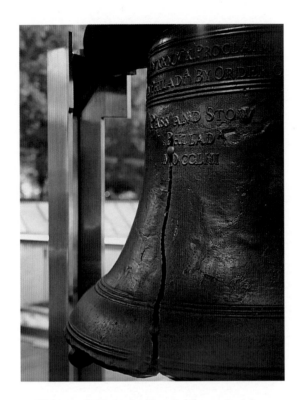

Titles available in the Pictorial Souvenir series